NBA CHAMPIONS MIAMI HEAT

AARON FRISCH

CREATIVE EDUCATION

Published by Creative Education
P.O. Box 227, Mankato, Minnesota 56002
Creative Education is an imprint of The Creative Company
www.thecreativecompany.us

Book and cover design by Blue Design (www.bluedes.com)
Art direction by Rita Marshall
Printed by Corporate Graphics in the United States of
America

Photographs by Alamy (Travelshots), Getty Images (Issac
Baldizon/NBAE, Victor Baldizon/NBAE, Andrew D.
Bernstein/NBAE, Nathaniel S. Butler/NBAE, Lou Capozzola/
NBAE, Fernando Medina/NBAE, John W. McDonough/
Sports Illustrated, Fernando Medina/NBAE, Greg Nelson/
Sports Illustrated, Jamie Squire), US Presswire (Mark J.
Rebilas)

Library of Congress Cataloging-in-Publication Data

Frisch, Aaron.
Miami Heat / by Aaron Frisch.
Includes bibliographical references and index.
Summary: A basic introduction to the Miami Heat
professional basketball team, including its formation in 1988,
great players such as Alonzo Mourning, championship, and
stars of today.
ISBN 978-1-60818-137-7
1. Miami Heat (Basketball team)—History—Juvenile
literature. I. Title.
GV885.52.M53F75 2012
796.323'6409759381—dc22   2010051566

CPSIA: 030111 PO1448

First edition
9 8 7 6 5 4 3 2 1

Cover: LeBron James
Page 2: Dwyane Wade
Right: Brian Grant
Page 6: Michael Beasley

TABLE OF CONTENTS

The Heat have played in AmericanAirlines Arena since 1999

Miami is a city in Florida. Miami is a hot city with many beaches and palm trees. It has an **arena** called AmericanAirlines Arena that is the home of a basketball team called the Heat.

Miami was built next to the beaches along the Atlantic Ocean

The Heat are part of the National Basketball Association (NBA). All the teams in the NBA try to win the **NBA Finals** to become world champions. The Heat play many games against teams called the Bobcats, Hawks, Magic, and Wizards.

In 1995, Glen Rice scored 56 points in 1 game for the Heat

The Heat started playing

in 1988. They lost their first 17

games in a row! But they got

better after they added players

like **sharpshooting** forward

Glen Rice in 1989.

Pat Riley was an NBA head coach for 24 seasons (11 in Miami)

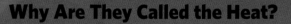

Why Are They Called the Heat?
Miami is one of the warmest cities in the United States. It is hot in the summer and stays warm in the winter. It almost never snows there, even in the winter.

From 1996 to 2001, coach Pat Riley led the Heat to the **playoffs** every year. Miami played many close, exciting playoff games against the New York Knicks. But the Heat could not get to the NBA Finals.

Dwyane Wade

HEAT FACTS

- Started playing: 1988

- Conference/division: Eastern Conference, Southeast Division

- Team colors: red, black, and orange

- NBA championship:

  2006 — 4 games to 2 versus Dallas Mavericks

- NBA Web site for kids: http://www.nba.com/kids/

In 2003, the Heat added fast guard Dwyane Wade. The next year, huge center Shaquille O'Neal came to Miami, too. These new stars made the Heat a tough team to beat.

SAY IT LIKE THIS

Shaquille
shuh-KEEL

Shaquille O'Neal was 7-foot-1 and weighed 325 pounds

In 2006, the Heat got to the NBA Finals. They lost the first two games to the Dallas Mavericks. But then Miami won the next four games to become world champions! People in Miami held a big parade to celebrate.

Many Heat fans wore all-white clothes to games in the 2006 NBA Finals

Heat stars Alonzo Mourning (above) and Rony Seikaly (opposite)

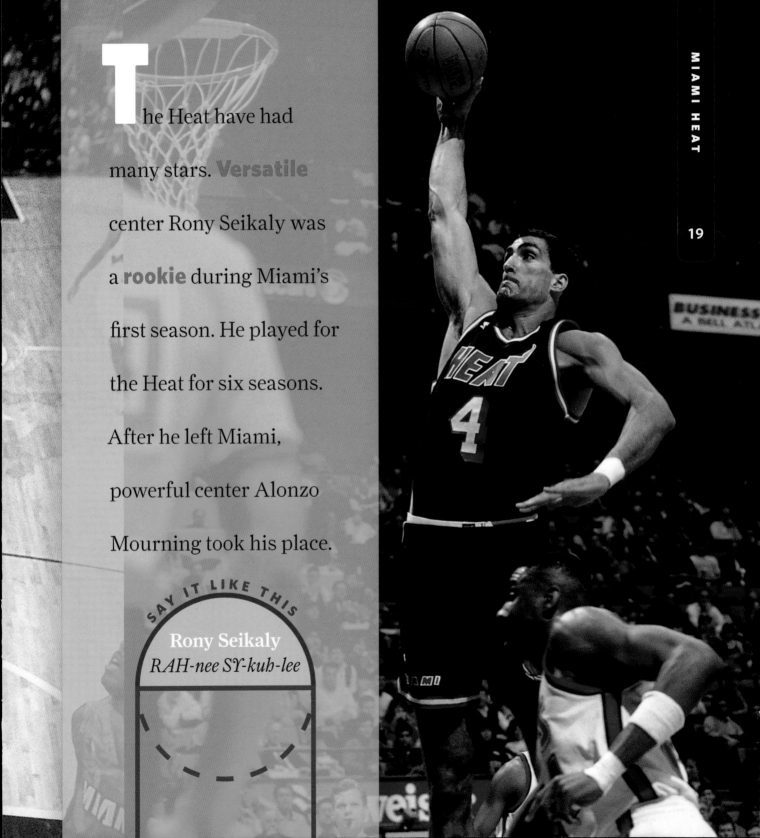

The Heat have had many stars. Versatile center Rony Seikaly was a rookie during Miami's first season. He played for the Heat for six seasons. After he left Miami, powerful center Alonzo Mourning took his place.

SAY IT LIKE THIS

Rony Seikaly
RAH-nee SY-kuh-lee

Eddie Jones played in Miami for six seasons

Tim Hardaway joined Miami in 1996. He was a quick point guard who liked to **drive** and then pass to teammates so they could score. Eddie Jones was another Heat star. He was a speedy guard.

It was hard to stop Tim Hardaway when he dribbled to the basket

LeBron James was so good that he was nicknamed "King James"

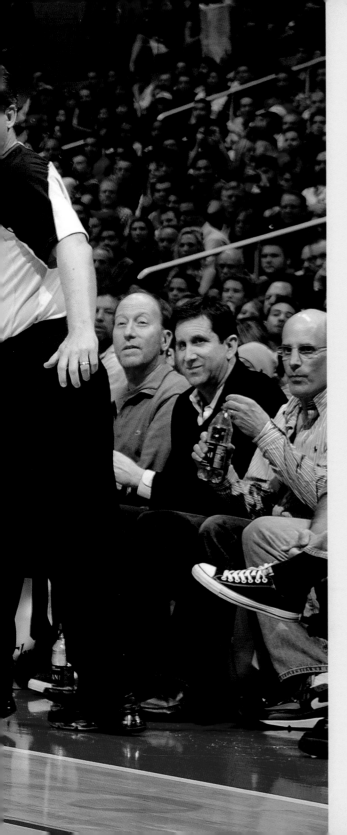

In 2010, Miami added LeBron James. He was a big forward who won awards as the best player in the NBA in 2009 and 2010. Miami fans hoped that he would help lead the Heat to their second NBA championship!

GLOSSARY

arena — a large building for indoor sports events; it has many seats for fans

drive — to dribble straight toward the basket, usually to try to get a close shot

NBA Finals — a series of games between two teams at the end of the playoffs; the first team to win four games is the champion

playoffs — games that the best teams play after a season

rookie — a player in his first season

sharpshooting — good at making shots from a long distance

versatile — able to do many different things well

INDEX